Job Hazard Analysis

U.S. Department of Labor
Occupational Safety and Health Administration
OSHA 3071
2002 (Revised)

Contents

Who needs to read this booklet?

This booklet is for employers, foremen, and supervisors, but we encourage employees to use the information as well to analyze their own jobs and recognize workplace hazards so they can report them to you. It explains what a job hazard analysis is and offers guidelines to help you conduct your own step-by-step analysis.

What is a hazard?

A hazard is the potential for harm. In practical terms, a hazard often is associated with a condition or activity that, if left uncontrolled, can result in an injury or illness. See Appendix 2 for a list of common hazards and descriptions. Identifying hazards and eliminating or controlling them as early as possible will help prevent injuries and illnesses.

What is a job hazard analysis?

A job hazard analysis is a technique that focuses on job tasks as a way to identify hazards before they occur. It focuses on the relationship between the worker, the task, the tools, and the work environment. Ideally, after you identify uncontrolled hazards, you will take steps to eliminate or reduce them to an acceptable risk level.

Why is job hazard analysis important?

Many workers are injured and killed at the workplace every day in the United States. Safety and health can add value to your business, your job, and your life. You can help prevent workplace injuries and illnesses by looking at your workplace operations, establishing proper job procedures, and ensuring that all employees are trained properly.

One of the best ways to determine and establish proper work procedures is to conduct a job hazard analysis. A job hazard analysis is one component of the larger commitment of a safety and health management system. (See page 15 for more information on safety and health management systems.)

What is the value of a job hazard analysis?

Supervisors can use the findings of a job hazard analysis to eliminate and prevent hazards in their workplaces. This is likely to result in fewer worker injuries and illnesses; safer, more effective work methods; reduced workers' compensation costs; and increased worker productivity. The analysis also can be a valuable tool for training new employees in the steps required to perform their jobs safely.

For a job hazard analysis to be effective, management must demonstrate its commitment to safety and health and follow through to correct any uncontrolled hazards identified. Otherwise, management will lose credibility and employees may hesitate to go to management when dangerous conditions threaten them.

What jobs are appropriate for a job hazard analysis?

A job hazard analysis can be conducted on many jobs in your workplace. Priority should go to the following types of jobs:

- Jobs with the highest injury or illness rates;

- Jobs with the potential to cause severe or disabling injuries or illness, even if there is no history of previous accidents;

- Jobs in which one simple human error could lead to a severe accident or injury;

- Jobs that are new to your operation or have undergone changes in processes and procedures; and

- Jobs complex enough to require written instructions.

Where do I begin?

1. **Involve your employees.** It is very important to involve your employees in the hazard analysis process. They have a unique understanding of the job, and this knowledge is invaluable for finding hazards. Involving employees will help minimize oversights, ensure a quality analysis, and get workers to "buy in" to the solutions because they will share ownership in their safety and health program.

2. **Review your accident history.** Review with your employees your worksite's history of accidents and occupational illnesses that needed treatment, losses that required repair or replacement, and any "near misses" — events in which an accident or loss did not occur,
but could have. These events are indicators that the existing hazard controls (if any) may not be adequate and deserve more scrutiny.

3. **Conduct a preliminary job review.** Discuss with your employees the hazards they know exist in their current work and surroundings. Brainstorm with them for ideas to eliminate or control those hazards.

   If any hazards exist that pose an immediate danger to an employee's life or health, take immediate action to protect the worker. Any problems that can be corrected easily should be corrected as soon as possible. Do not wait to complete your job hazard analysis. This will demonstrate your commitment to safety and health and enable you to focus on the hazards and jobs that need more study because of their complexity. For those hazards determined to present unacceptable risks, evaluate types of hazard controls. More information about hazard controls is found in Appendix 1.

4. **List, rank, and set priorities for hazardous jobs.** List jobs with hazards that present unacceptable risks, based on those most likely to occur and with the most severe consequences. These jobs should be your first priority for analysis.

5. **Outline the steps or tasks.** Nearly every job can be broken down into job tasks or steps. When beginning a job hazard analysis, watch the employee perform the job and list each step as the worker takes it. Be sure to record enough information to describe each job action without getting overly detailed. Avoid making the breakdown of steps so detailed that it becomes unnecessarily long or so broad that it does not include basic steps. You may find it valuable to get input from other workers who have performed the same job. Later, review the job steps with the employee to make sure you have not omitted something. Point out that you are evaluating the job itself, not the employee's job performance. Include the employee in all phases of the analysis—from reviewing the job steps and procedures to discussing uncontrolled hazards and recommended solutions.

Sometimes, in conducting a job hazard analysis, it may be helpful to photograph or videotape the worker performing the job. These visual records can be handy references when doing a more detailed analysis of the work.

How do I identify workplace hazards?

A job hazard analysis is an exercise in detective work. Your goal is to discover the following:

- What can go wrong?
- What are the consequences?
- How could it arise?
- What are other contributing factors?
- How likely is it that the hazard will occur?

To make your job hazard analysis useful, document the answers to these questions in a consistent manner. Describing a hazard in this way helps to ensure that your efforts to eliminate the hazard and implement hazard controls help target the most important contributors to the hazard.

Good hazard scenarios describe:

- Where it is happening (environment),
- Who or what it is happening to (exposure),
- What precipitates the hazard (trigger),
- The outcome that would occur should it happen (consequence), and
- Any other contributing factors.

A sample form found in Appendix 3 helps you organize your information to provide these details.

Rarely is a hazard a simple case of one singular cause resulting in one singular effect. More frequently, many contributing factors tend to line up in a certain way to create the hazard. Here is an example of a hazard scenario:

In the metal shop (environment), while clearing a snag (trigger), a worker's hand (exposure) comes into contact with a rotating pulley. It pulls his hand into the machine and severs his fingers (consequences) quickly.

To perform a job hazard analysis, you would ask:

- **What can go wrong?** The worker's hand could come into contact with a rotating object that "catches" it and pulls it into the machine.

- **What are the consequences?** The worker could receive a severe injury and lose fingers and hands.

- **How could it happen?** The accident could happen as a result of the worker trying to clear a snag during operations or as part of a maintenance activity while the pulley is operating. Obviously, this hazard scenario could not occur
if the pulley is not rotating.

- **What are other contributing factors?** This hazard occurs very quickly. It does not give the worker much opportunity to recover or prevent it once his hand comes into contact with the pulley. This is an important factor, because it helps you determine the severity and likelihood of an accident when selecting appropriate hazard controls. Unfortunately, experience has shown that training is not very effective in hazard control when triggering events happen quickly because humans can react only so quickly.

- **How likely is it that the hazard will occur?** This determination requires some judgment. If there have been "near-misses" or actual cases, then the likelihood of a recurrence would be considered high. If the pulley is exposed and easily accessible, that also is a consideration. In the example, the likelihood that the hazard will occur is high because there is no guard preventing contact, and the operation is performed while the machine is running. By following the steps in this example, you can organize your hazard analysis activities.

The examples that follow show how a job hazard analysis can be used to identify the existing or potential hazards for each basic step involved in grinding iron castings.

Grinding Iron Castings: Job Steps

Step 1. Reach into metal box to right of machine, grasp casting, and carry to wheel.

Step 2. Push casting against wheel to grind off burr.

Step 3. Place finished casting in box to left of machine.

Example Job Hazard Analysis Form

Job Location:	*Analyst*:	*Date*:
Metal Shop	Joe Safety	

Task Description: Worker reaches into metal box to the right of the machine, grasps a 15-pound casting and carries it to grinding wheel. Worker grinds 20 to 30 castings per hour.

Hazard Description: Picking up a casting, the employee could drop it onto his foot. The casting's weight and height could seriously injure the worker's foot or toes.

Hazard Controls:

1. Remove castings from the box and place them on a table next to the grinder.

2. Wear steel-toe shoes with arch protection.

3. Change protective gloves that allow a better grip.

4. Use a device to pick up castings.

Job Location:	**Analyst:**	**Date:**
Metal Shop	Joe Safety	

Task Description: Worker reaches into metal box to the right of the machine, grasps a 15-pound casting and carries it to grinding wheel. Worker grinds 20 to 30 castings per hour.

Hazard Description: Castings have sharp burrs and edges that can cause severe lacerations.

Hazard Controls:

1. Use a device such as a clamp to pick up castings.

2. Wear cut-resistant gloves that allow a good grip and fit tightly to minimize the chance that they will get caught in grinding wheel.

Job Location:	Analyst:	Date:
Metal Shop	Joe Safety	

Task Description: Worker reaches into metal box to the right of the machine, grasps a 15-pound casting and carries it to grinding wheel. Worker grinds 20 to 30 castings per hour.

Hazard Description: Reaching, twisting, and lifting 15-pound castings from the floor could result in a muscle strain to the lower back.

Hazard Controls:

1. Move castings from the ground and place them closer to the work zone to minimize lifting. Ideally, place them at waist height or on an adjustable platform or pallet.

2. Train workers not to twist while lifting and reconfigure work stations to minimize twisting during lifts.

Repeat similar forms for each job step.

11

How do I correct or prevent hazards?

After reviewing your list of hazards with the employee, consider what control methods will eliminate or reduce them. For more information on hazard control measures, see Appendix 1. The most effective controls are engineering controls that physically change a machine or work environment to prevent employee exposure to the hazard. The more reliable or less likely a hazard control can be circumvented, the better. If this is not feasible, administrative controls may be appropriate. This may involve changing how employees do their jobs.

Discuss your recommendations with all employees who perform the job and consider their responses carefully. If you plan to introduce new or modified job procedures, be sure they understand what they are required to do and the reasons for the changes.

What else do I need to know before starting a job hazard analysis?

The job procedures discussed in this booklet are for illustration only and do not necessarily include all the steps, hazards, and protections that apply to your industry. When conducting your own job safety analysis, be sure to consult the Occupational Safety and Health Administration standards for your industry. Compliance with these standards is mandatory, and by incorporating their requirements in your job hazard analysis, you can be sure that your health and safety program meets federal standards. OSHA standards, regulations, and technical information are available online at www.osha.gov.

Twenty-four states and two territories operate their own OSHA-approved safety and health programs and may have standards that differ slightly from federal requirements. Employers in those states should check with the appropriate state agency for more information. A list of applicable states and territories and contact information is provided on page 32.

Why should I review my job hazard analysis?

Periodically reviewing your job hazard analysis ensures that it remains current and continues to help reduce workplace accidents and injuries. Even if the job has not changed, it is possible that during the review process you will identify hazards that were not identified in the initial analysis.

It is particularly important to review your job hazard analysis if an illness or injury occurs on a specific job. Based on the circumstances, you may determine that you need to change the job procedure to prevent similar incidents in the future. If an employee's failure to follow proper job procedures results in a "close call," discuss the situation with all employees who perform the job and remind them of proper procedures. Any time you revise a job hazard analysis, it is important to train all employees affected by the changes in the new job methods, procedures, or protective measures adopted.

When is it appropriate to hire a professional to conduct a job hazard analysis?

If your employees are involved in many different or complex processes, you need professional help conducting your job hazard analyses. Sources of help include your insurance company, the local fire department, and private consultants with safety and health expertise. In addition, OSHA offers assistance through its regional and area offices and consultation services. Contact numbers are listed at the back of this publication.

Even when you receive outside help, it is important that you and your employees remain involved in the process of identifying and correcting hazards because you are on the worksite every day and most likely to encounter these hazards. New circumstances and a recombination of existing circumstances may cause old hazards to reappear and new hazards to appear. In addition, you and your employees must be ready and able to implement whatever hazard elimination or control measures a professional consultant recommends.

OSHA Assistance, Services, and Programs

How can OSHA help me?

OSHA can provide extensive help through a variety of programs, including assistance about safety and health programs, state plans, workplace consultations, Voluntary Protection Programs, strategic partnerships, training and education, and more.

How does safety and health program management assistance help employers and employees?

Effective management of worker safety and health protection is a decisive factor in reducing the extent and severity of work-related injuries and illnesses and their related costs. In fact, an effective safety and health program forms the basis of good worker protection and can save time and money—about $4 for every dollar spent—and increase productivity.

To assist employers and employees in developing effective safety and health systems, OSHA published recommended *Safety and Health Program Management Guidelines,* (*Federal Register* 54(18):3908–3916, January 26, 1989). These voluntary guidelines can be applied to all worksites covered by OSHA.

The guidelines identify four general elements that are critical to the development of a successful safety and health management program:

- Management leadership and employee involvement;

- Worksite analysis;

- Hazard prevention and control; and

- Safety and health training.

The guidelines recommend specific actions under each of these general elements to achieve an effective safety and health program. The *Federal Register* notice is available online at www.osha.gov.

What are state plans?

State plans are OSHA-approved job safety and health programs operated by individual states or territories instead of Federal OSHA. The *Occupational Safety and Health Act of 1970 (OSH Act)* encourages states to develop and operate their own job safety and health plans and permits state enforcement of OSHA standards if the state has an approved plan. Once OSHA approves a state plan, it funds 50 percent of the program's operating costs. State plans must provide standards and enforcement programs, as well as voluntary compliance activities, that are at least as effective as those of Federal OSHA.

There are 26 state plans: 23 cover both private and public (state and local government) employment, and 3 (Connecticut, New Jersey, and New York) cover only the public sector. For more information on state plans, see the listing at the end of this publication, or visit OSHA's website at www.osha.gov.

How can consultation assistance help employers?

In addition to helping employers identify and correct specific hazards, OSHA's consultation service provides free, onsite assistance in developing and implementing effective workplace safety and health management systems that emphasize the prevention of worker injuries and illnesses.

Comprehensive consultation assistance provided by OSHA includes a hazard survey of the worksite and an appraisal of all aspects of the employer's existing safety and health management system. In addition, the service offers assistance to employers in developing and implementing an effective safety and health management system. Employers also may receive training and education services, as well as limited assistance away from the worksite.

Who can get consultation assistance and what does it cost?

Consultation assistance is available to small employers (with fewer than 250 employees at a fixed site and no more than 500 corporatewide) who want help in establishing and maintaining a safe and healthful workplace.

Funded largely by OSHA, the service is provided at no cost to the employer. Primarily developed for smaller employers with more hazardous operations, the consultation service is delivered by state governments employing professional safety and health consultants. No penalties are proposed or citations issued for hazards identified by the consultant. The employer's only obligation is to correct all identified serious hazards within the agreed-upon correction time frame.

Can OSHA assure privacy to an employer who asks for consultation assistance?

OSHA provides consultation assistance to the employer with the assurance that his or her name and firm and any information about the workplace will not be routinely reported to OSHA enforcement staff.

Can an employer be cited for violations after receiving consultation assistance?

If an employer fails to eliminate or control a serious hazard within the agreed-upon time frame, the Consultation Project Manager must refer the situation to the OSHA enforcement office for appropriate action. This is a rare occurrence, however, since employers request the service for the expressed purpose of identifying and fixing hazards in their workplaces.

Does OSHA provide any incentives for seeking consultation assistance?

Yes. Under the consultation program, certain exemplary employers may request participation in OSHA's Safety and Health Achievement Recognition Program (SHARP). Eligibility for participation in SHARP includes, but is not limited to, receiving a full-service, comprehensive consultation visit, correcting all identified hazards, and developing an effective safety and health management system.

Employers accepted into SHARP may receive an exemption from programmed inspections (not complaint or accident investigation inspections) for a period of 1 year initially, or 2 years upon renewal.

For more information concerning consultation assistance, see the list of consultation offices beginning on page 36, contact your regional or area OSHA office, or visit OSHA's website at www.osha.gov.

What are the Voluntary Protection Programs?

Voluntary Protection Programs (VPPs) represent one part of OSHA's effort to extend worker protection beyond the minimum required by OSHA standards. VPP—along with onsite consultation services, full-service area offices, and OSHA's Strategic Partnership Program (OSPP)—represents a cooperative approach which, when coupled with an effective enforcement program, expands worker protection to help meet the goals of the *OSH Act.*

How does VPP work?

There are three levels of VPP recognition: Star, Merit, and Demonstration. All are designed to do the following:

- Recognize employers who have successfully developed and implemented effective and comprehensive safety and health management systems;

- Encourage these employers to continuously improve their safety and health management systems;

- Motivate other employers to achieve excellent safety and health results in the same outstanding way; and

- Establish a relationship between employers, employees, and OSHA that is based on cooperation.

How does VPP help employers and employees?

VPP participation can mean the following:

- Reduced numbers of worker fatalities, injuries, and illnesses;

- Lost-workday case rates generally 50 percent below industry averages;

- Lower workers' compensation and other injury- and illness-related costs;

- Improved employee motivation to work safely, leading to a better quality of life at work;

- Positive community recognition and interaction;

- Further improvement and revitalization of already-good safety and health programs; and a

- Positive relationship with OSHA.

How does OSHA monitor VPP sites?

OSHA reviews an employer's VPP application and conducts a VPP Onsite Evaluation to verify that the safety and health management systems described are operating effectively at the site. OSHA conducts Onsite Evaluations on a regular basis, annually for participants at the Demonstration level, every 18 months for Merit, and every 3 to 5 years for Star. Each February, all participants must send a copy of their most recent Annual Evaluation to their OSHA regional office. This evaluation must include the worksite's record of injuries and illnesses for the past year.

Can OSHA inspect an employer who is participating in the VPP?

Sites participating in VPP are not scheduled for regular, programmed inspections. OSHA handles any employee complaints, serious accidents, or significant chemical releases that may occur at VPP sites according to routine enforcement procedures.

Additional information on VPP is available from OSHA national, regional, and area offices, listed beginning on page 27. Also, see **Outreach** at OSHA's website at www.osha.gov.

How can a partnership with OSHA improve worker safety and health?

OSHA has learned firsthand that voluntary, cooperative partnerships with employers, employees, and unions can be a useful alternative to traditional enforcement and an effective way to reduce worker deaths, injuries, and illnesses. This is especially true when a partnership leads to the development and implementation of a comprehensive workplace safety and health management system.

What is OSHA's Strategic Partnership Program (OSPP)?

OSHA Strategic Partnerships are alliances among labor, management, and government to foster improvements in workplace safety and health. These partnerships are voluntary, cooperative relationships between OSHA, employers, employee representatives, and others such as trade unions, trade and professional associations, universities, and other government agencies. OSPPs are the newest member of OSHA's family of cooperative programs.

What do OSPPs do?

These partnerships encourage, assist, and recognize the efforts of the partners to eliminate serious workplace hazards and achieve a high level of worker safety and health. Whereas OSHA's Consultation Program and VPP entail one-on-one relationships between OSHA and individual worksites, most strategic partnerships seek to have a broader impact by building cooperative relationships with groups of employers and employees.

What are the different kinds of OSPPs?

There are two major types:

• Comprehensive, which focuses on establishing comprehensive safety and health management systems at partnering worksites; and

• Limited, which helps identify and eliminate hazards associated with worker deaths, injuries, and illnesses, or have goals other than establishing comprehensive worksite safety and health programs.

OSHA is interested in creating new OSPPs at the national, regional, and local levels. OSHA also has found limited partnerships to be valuable. Limited partnerships might address the elimination or control of a specific industry hazard.

What are the benefits of participation in the OSPP?

Like VPP, OSPP can mean the following:

• Fewer worker fatalities, injuries, and illnesses;

• Lower workers' compensation and other injury- and illness-related costs;

• Improved employee motivation to work safely, leading to a better quality of life at work and enhanced productivity;

- Positive community recognition and interaction;

- Development of or improvement in safety and health management systems; and

- Positive interaction with OSHA.

For more information about this program, contact your nearest OSHA office or go to the agency website at www.osha.gov.

Does OSHA have occupational safety and health training for employers and employees?

Yes. The OSHA Training Institute in Des Plaines, IL, provides basic and advanced training and education in safety and health for federal and state compliance officers, state consultants, other federal agency personnel, and private-sector employers, employees, and their representatives.

Institute courses cover diverse safety and health topics including electrical hazards, machine guarding, personal protective equipment, ventilation, and ergonomics. The facility includes classrooms, laboratories, a library, and an audiovisual unit. The laboratories contain various demonstrations and equipment, such as power presses, woodworking and welding shops, a complete industrial ventilation unit, and a sound demonstration laboratory. More than 57 courses dealing with subjects such as safety and health in the construction industry and methods of compliance with OSHA standards are available for personnel in the private sector.

In addition, OSHA's 73 area offices are full-service centers offering a variety of informational services such as personnel for speaking engagements, publications, audiovisual aids on workplace hazards, and technical advice.

Does OSHA give money to organizations for training and education?

OSHA awards grants through its Susan Harwood Training Grant Program to nonprofit organizations to provide safety and health training and education to employers and workers in the workplace. The grants focus on programs that will educate workers and employers in small business (fewer than 250 employees), train workers and employers about new OSHA standards or high-risk activities or hazards. Grants are awarded for 1 year and may be renewed for an additional 12 months depending on whether the grantee has performed satisfactorily.

OSHA expects each organization awarded a grant to develop a training and/or education program that addresses a safety and health topic named by OSHA, recruit workers and employers for the training, and conduct the training. Grantees are also expected to follow-up with people who have been trained to find out what changes were made to reduce the hazards in their workplaces as a result of the training.

Each year OSHA has a national competition that is announced in the *Federal Register* and on the Internet at www.osha-slc.gov/Training/sharwood/sharwood.html. If you do not have access to the Internet, you can contact the OSHA Office of Training and Education, 1555 Times Drive, Des Plaines, IL 60018, (847) 297–4810, for more information.

Does OSHA have other assistance materials available?

Yes. OSHA has a variety of materials and tools available on its website at www.osha.gov. These include eTools, Expert Advisors, Electronic Compliance Assistance Tools (e-CATs), Technical Links, regulations, directives, publications, videos, and other information for employers and employees. OSHA's software programs and compliance assistance tools walk you through challenging safety and health issues and common problems to find the best solutions for your workplace. OSHA's comprehensive publications program includes more than 100 titles to help you understand OSHA requirements and programs.

OSHA's CD-ROM includes standards, interpretations, directives, and more and can be purchased on CD-ROM from the U.S. Government Printing Office. To order, write to the Superintendent of Documents, U.S. Government Printing Office, Washington, DC 20402, or phone (202) 512–1800. Specify *OSHA Regulations, Documents and Technical Information on CD-ROM (ORDT)*, GPO Order No. S/N 729-013-00000-5.

What other publications does OSHA offer?

OSHA offers more than 100 documents, including brochures, fact sheets, posters, pocket cards, flyers, technical documents, and a quarterly magazine. These documents are available online at www.osha.gov or by calling (202) 693–1888.

What do I do in case of an emergency or if I need to file a complaint?

To report an emergency, file a complaint, or seek OSHA advice, assistance, or products, call (800) 321–OSHA or contact your nearest OSHA regional or area office listed beginning on page 27. The teletypewriter (TTY) number is (877) 889–5627.

You can also file a complaint online and obtain more information on OSHA federal and state programs by visiting OSHA's website at www.osha.gov.

For more information on grants, training, and education, write: OSHA Training Institute, Office of Training and Education, 1555 Times Drive, Des Plaines, IL 60018; call (847) 297–4810; or see Outreach on OSHA's website at www.osha.gov.

OSHA Regional and Area Offices

OSHA Regional Offices

Region I
(CT,* ME, MA, NH, RI, VT*)
JFK Federal Building, Room E340
Boston, MA 02203
(617) 565–9860

Region II
(NJ,* NY,* PR,* VI*)
201 Varick Street, Room 670
New York, NY 10014
(212) 337–2378

Region III
(DE, DC, MD,* PA,* VA,* WV)
The Curtis Center
170 S. Independence Mall West
Suite 740 West
Philadelphia, PA 19106-3309
(215) 861–4900

Region IV
(AL, FL, GA, KY,* MS, NC,*
SC,* TN*)
Atlanta Federal Center
61 Forsyth Street, SW, Room 6T50
Atlanta, GA 30303
(404) 562–2300

Region V
(IL, IN,* MI,* MN,* OH, WI)
230 South Dearborn Street
Room 3244
Chicago, IL 60604
(312) 353–2220

Region VI
(AR, LA, NM,* OK, TX)
525 Griffin Street, Room 602
Dallas, TX 75202
(214) 767–4731 or 4736 x224

Region VII
(IA,* KS, MO, NE)
City Center Square
1100 Main Street, Suite 800
Kansas City, MO 64105
(816) 426–5861

Region VIII
(CO, MT, ND, SD, UT,* WY*)
1999 Broadway, Suite 1690
Denver, CO 80202-5716
(303) 844–1600

Region IX
(American Samoa, AZ,*
CA,* HI, NV,* Northern
Mariana Islands)
71 Stevenson Street, Room 420
San Francisco, CA 94105
(415) 975–4310

Region X
(AK,* ID, OR,* WA*)
1111 Third Avenue, Suite 715
Seattle, WA 98101-3212
(206) 553–5930

---

*These states and territories operate their own OSHA-approved
job safety and health programs (Connecticut, New Jersey and
New York plans cover public employees only). States with
approved programs must have a standard that is identical to,
or at least as effective as, the federal standard.

27

OSHA Area Offices

Birmingham, AL
(205) 731–1534

Mobile, AL
(251) 441–6131

Anchorage, AK
(907) 271–5152

Little Rock, AR
(501) 324–6291(5818)

Phoenix, AZ
(602) 640–2348

San Diego, CA
(619) 557–5909

Sacramento, CA
(916) 566–7471

Denver, CO
(303) 844–5285

Greenwood Village, CO
(303) 843–4500

Bridgeport, CT
(203) 579–5581

Hartford, CT
(860) 240–3152

Wilmington, DE
(302) 573–6518

Fort Lauderdale, FL
(954) 424–0242

Jacksonville, FL
(904) 232–2895

Tampa, FL
(813) 626–1177

Savannah, GA
(912) 652–4393

Smyrna, GA
(770) 984–8700

Tucker, GA
(770) 493–6644/6742/8419

Des Moines, IA
(515) 284–4794

Boise, ID
(208) 321–2960

Calumet City, IL
(708) 891–3800

Des Plaines, IL
(847) 803–4800

Fairview Heights, IL
(618) 632–8612

North Aurora, IL
(630) 896–8700

Peoria, IL
(309) 671–7033

Indianapolis, IN
(317) 226–7290

Wichita, KS
(316) 269–6644

Jackson, MS
(601) 965–4606

Frankfort, KY
(502) 227–7024

Billings, MT
(406) 247–7494

Baton Rouge, LA
(225) 389–0474 (0431)

Raleigh, NC
(919) 856–4770

Braintree, MA
(617) 565–6924

Omaha, NE
(402) 221–3182

Methuen, MA
(617) 565–8110

Bismark, ND
(701) 250–4521

Springfield, MA
(413) 785–0123

Concord, NH
(603) 225–1629

Linthicum, MD
(410) 865–2055/2056

Avenel, NJ
(732) 750–3270

Bangor, ME
(207) 941–8177

Hasbrouck Heights, NJ
(201) 288–1700

Portland, ME
(207) 780–3178

Marlton, NJ
(856) 757–5181

August, ME
(207) 622–8417

Parsippany, NJ
(973) 263–1003

Lansing, MI
(517) 327–0904

Carson City, NV
(775) 885–6963

Minneapolis, MN
(612) 664–5460

Albany, NY
(518) 464–4338

Kansas City, MO
(816) 483–9531

Bayside, NY
(718) 279–9060

St. Louis, MO
(314) 425–4249

Bowmansville, NY
(716) 684–3891

New York, NY
(212) 337-2636

North Syracuse, NY
(315) 451-0808

Tarrytown, NY
(914) 524-7510

Westbury, NY
(516) 334-3344

Cincinnati, OH
(513) 841-4132

Cleveland, OH
(216) 522-3818

Columbus, OH
(614) 469-5582

Toledo, OH
(419) 259-7542

Oklahoma City, OK
(405) 278-9560

Portland, OR
(503) 326-2251

Allentown, PA
(610) 776-0592

Erie, PA
(814) 833-5758

Harrisburg, PA
(717) 782-3902

Philadelphia, PA
(215) 597-4955

Pittsburgh, PA
(412) 395-4903

Wilkes-Barre, PA
(570) 826-6538

Guaynabo, PR
(787) 277-1560

Providence, RI
(401) 528-4669

Columbia, SC
(803) 765-5904

Nashville, TN
(615) 781-5423

Austin, TX
(512) 916-5783 (5788)

Corpus Christi, TX
(361) 888-3420

Dallas, TX
(214) 320-2400 (2558)

El Paso, TX
(915) 534-6251

Fort Worth, TX
(817) 428-2470 (485-7647)

Houston, TX
(281) 591-2438 (2787)

Houston, TX
(281) 286-0583/0584 (5922)

Lubbock, TX
(806) 472-7681 (7685)

Salt Lake City, UT
(801) 530–6901

Norfolk, VA
(757) 441–3820

Bellevue, WA
(206) 553–7520

Appleton, WI
(920) 734–4521

Eau Claire, WI
(715) 832–9019

Madison, WI
(608) 264–5388

Milwaukee, WI
(414) 297–3315

Charleston, WV
(304) 347–5937

OSHA-Approved Safety and Health Plans

Alaska

Alaska Department of Labor
and Workforce Development

Commissioner
(907) 465–2700
FAX: (907) 465–2784

Program Director
(907) 269–4904
FAX: (907) 269–4915

Arizona

Industrial Commission
of Arizona

Director, ICA
(602) 542–4411
FAX: (602) 542–1614

Program Director
(602) 542–5795
FAX: (602) 542–1614

California

California Department of
Industrial Relations

Director
(415) 703–5050
FAX: (415) 703–5114

Chief
(415) 703–5100
FAX: (415) 703–5114

Manager, Cal/OSHA
Program Office
(415) 703–5177
FAX: (415) 703–5114

Connecticut

Connecticut Department
of Labor

Commissioner
(860) 566–5123
FAX: (860) 566–1520

Conn-OSHA Director
(860) 566–4550
FAX: (860) 566–6916

Hawaii

Hawaii Department of Labor
and Industrial Relations

Director
(808) 586–8844
FAX: (808) 586–9099

Administrator
(808) 586–9116
FAX: (808) 586–9104

Indiana

Indiana Department of Labor

Commissioner
(317) 232–2378
FAX: (317) 233–3790

Deputy Commissioner
(317) 232–3325
FAX: (317) 233–3790

Iowa

Iowa Division of Labor

Commissioner
(515) 281–6432
FAX: (515) 281–4698

Administrator
(515) 281–3469
FAX: (515) 281–7995

Kentucky

Kentucky Labor Cabinet
Secretary (502) 564–3070
FAX: (502) 564–5387

Federal\State Coordinator
(502) 564–3070 ext.240
FAX: (502) 564–1682

Maryland

Maryland Division of Labor
and Industry

Commissioner
(410) 767–2999
FAX: (410) 767–2300

Deputy Commissioner
(410) 767–2992
FAX: (410) 767–2003

Assistant Commissioner, MOSH
(410) 767–2215
FAX: (410) 767–2003

Michigan

Michigan Department of
Consumer and Industry Services

Director
(517) 322–1814
FAX: (517) 322–1775

Minnesota

Minnesota Department of
Labor and Industry

Commissioner
(651) 296–2342
FAX: (651) 282–5405

Assistant Commissioner
(651) 296–6529
FAX: (651) 282–5293

Administrative Director,
OSHA Management Team
(651) 282–5772
FAX: (651) 297–2527

Nevada

Nevada Division of
Industrial Relations

Administrator
(775) 687–3032
FAX: (775) 687–6305

Chief Administrative Officer
(702) 486–9044
FAX: (702) 990–0358
[Las Vegas (702) 687–5240]

New Jersey

New Jersey Department of Labor

Commissioner
(609) 292–2975
FAX: (609) 633–9271

Assistant Commissioner
(609) 292–2313
FAX: (609) 292–1314

Program Director, PEOSH
(609) 292–3923
FAX: (609) 292–4409

33

New Mexico

New Mexico Environment
Department

Secretary
(505) 827–2850
FAX: (505) 827–2836

Chief
(505) 827–4230
FAX: (505) 827–4422

New York

New York Department of Labor

Acting Commissioner
(518) 457–2741
FAX: (518) 457–6908

Division Director
(518) 457–3518
FAX: (518) 457–6908

North Carolina

North Carolina Department
of Labor

Commissioner
(919) 807–2900
FAX: (919) 807–2855

Deputy Commissioner,
OSH Director
(919) 807–2861
FAX: (919) 807–2855

OSH Assistant Director
(919) 807–2863
FAX: (919) 807–2856

Oregon

Oregon Occupational Safety
and Health Division

Administrator
(503) 378–3272
FAX: (503) 947–7461

Deputy Administrator for Policy
(503) 378–3272
FAX: (503) 947–7461

Deputy Administrator
for Operations
(503) 378–3272
FAX: (503) 947–7461

Puerto Rico

Puerto Rico Department of
Labor and Human Resources

Secretary
(787) 754–2119
FAX: (787) 753–9550

Assistant Secretary for
Occupational Safety and Health
(787) 756–1100,
1106 / 754–2171
FAX: (787) 767–6051

Deputy Director for
Occupational Safety and Health
(787) 756–1100/1106,
754–2188
FAX: (787) 767–6051

South Carolina

South Carolina Department of
Labor, Licensing, and
Regulation

Director
(803) 896–4300
FAX: (803) 896–4393

Program Director
(803) 734–9644
FAX: (803) 734–9772

Tennessee

Tennessee Department of Labor

Commissioner
(615) 741–2582
FAX: (615) 741–5078

Acting Program Director
(615) 741–2793
FAX: (615) 741–3325

Utah

Utah Labor Commission

Commissioner
(801) 530–6901
FAX: (801) 530–7906

Administrator
(801) 530–6898
FAX: (801) 530–6390

Vermont

Vermont Department of
Labor and Industry

Commissioner
(802) 828–2288
FAX: (802) 828–2748

Project Manager
(802) 828–2765
FAX: (802) 828–2195

Virgin Islands

Virgin Islands Department
of Labor

Acting Commissioner
(340) 773–1990
FAX: (340) 773–1858

Program Director
(340) 772–1315
FAX: (340) 772–4323

Virginia

Virginia Department of Labor
and Industry

Commissioner
(804) 786–2377
FAX: (804) 371–6524

Director, Office of Legal Support
(804) 786–9873
FAX: (804) 786–8418

Washington

Washington Department of
Labor and Industries

Director
(360) 902–4200
FAX: (360) 902–4202

Assistant Director
(360) 902–5495
FAX: (360) 902–5529

Program Manager,
Federal–State Operations
(360) 902–5430
FAX: (360) 902–5529

Wyoming

Wyoming Department of
Employment

Safety Administrator
(307) 777–7786
FAX: (307) 777–3646

OSHA Consultation Projects

Anchorage, AK
(907) 269-4957

Boise, ID
(208) 426-3283

Tuscaloosa, AL
(205) 348-3033

Chicago, IL
(312) 814-2337

Little Rock, AR
(501) 682-4522

Indianapolis, IN
(317) 232-2688

Phoenix, AZ
(602) 542-1695

Topeka, KS
(785) 296-2251

Sacramento, CA
(916) 263-2856

Frankfort, KY
(502) 564-6895

Fort Collins, CO
(970) 491-6151

Baton Rouge, LA
(225) 342-9601

Wethersfield, CT
(860) 566-4550

West Newton, MA
(617) 727-3982

Washington, DC
(202) 541-3727

Laurel, MD
(410) 880-4970

Wilmington, DE
(302) 761-8219

Augusta, ME
(207) 624-6400

Tampa, FL
(813) 974-9962

Lansing, MI
(517) 322-1809

Atlanta, GA
(404) 894-2643

Saint Paul, MN
(651) 284-5060

Tiyam, GU
9-1-(671) 475-1101

Jefferson City, MO
(573) 751-3403

Honolulu, HI
(808) 586-9100

Pearl, MS
(601) 939-2047

Des Moines, IA
(515) 281-7629

Helena, MT
(406) 444-6418

Raleigh, NC
(919) 807–2905

Columbia, SC
(803) 734–9614

Bismarck, ND
(701) 328–5188

Brookings, SD
(605) 688–4101

Lincoln, NE
(402) 471–4717

Nashville, TN
(615) 741–7036

Concord, NH
(603) 271–2024

Austin, TX
(512) 804–4640

Trenton, NJ
(609) 292–3923

Salt Lake City, UT
(801) 530–6901

Santa Fe, NM
(505) 827–4230

Montpelier, VT
(802) 828–2765

Albany, NY
(518) 457–2238

Richmond, VA
(804) 786–6359

Henderson, NV
(702) 486–9140

Christiansted St. Croix, VI
(809) 772–1315

Columbus, OH
(614) 644–2631

Olympia, WA
(360) 902–5638

Oklahoma City, OK
(405) 528–1500

Madison, WI
(608) 266–9383

Salem, OR
(503) 378–3272

Waukesha, WI
(262) 523–3044

Indiana, PA
(724) 357–2396

Charleston, WV
(304) 558–7890

Hato Rey, PR
(787) 754–2171

Cheyenne, WY
(307) 777–7786

Providence, RI
(401) 222–2438

Appendices

Appendix 1
Hazard Control Measures

Information obtained from a job hazard analysis is useless unless hazard control measures recommended in the analysis are incorporated into the tasks. Managers should recognize that not all hazard controls are equal. Some are more effective than others at reducing the risk.

The order of precedence and effectiveness of hazard control is the following:

1. Engineering controls.

2. Administrative controls.

3. Personal protective equipment.

Engineering controls include the following:

- Elimination/minimization of the hazard—Designing the facility, equipment, or process to remove the hazard, or substituting processes, equipment, materials, or other factors to lessen the hazard;

- Enclosure of the hazard using enclosed cabs, enclosures for noisy equipment, or other means;

- Isolation of the hazard with interlocks, machine guards, blast shields, welding curtains, or other means; and

- Removal or redirection of the hazard such as with local and exhaust ventilation.

Administrative controls include the following:

- Written operating procedures, work permits, and safe work practices;

- Exposure time limitations (used most commonly to control temperature extremes and ergonomic hazards);

- Monitoring the use of highly hazardous materials;

- Alarms, signs, and warnings;

- Buddy system; and

- Training.

Personal Protective Equipment—such as respirators, hearing protection, protective clothing, safety glasses, and hardhats—is acceptable as a control method in the following circumstances:

- When engineering controls are not feasible or do not totally eliminate the hazard;

- While engineering controls are being developed;

- When safe work practices do not provide sufficient additional protection; and

- During emergencies when engineering controls may not be feasible.

Use of one hazard control method over another higher in the control precedence may be appropriate for providing interim protection until the hazard is abated permanently. In reality, if the hazard cannot be eliminated entirely, the adopted control measures will likely be a combination of all three items instituted simultaneously.

Appendix 2
Common Hazards and Descriptions

Hazards	Hazard Descriptions
Chemical (Toxic)	A chemical that exposes a person by absorption through the skin, inhalation, or through the blood stream that causes illness, disease, or death. The amount of chemical exposure is critical in determining hazardous effects. Check Material Safety Data Sheets (MSDS), and/or OSHA 1910.1000 for chemical hazard information.
Chemical (Flammable)	A chemical that, when exposed to a heat ignition source, results in combustion. Typically, the lower a chemical's flash point and boiling point, the more flammable the chemical. Check MSDS for flammability information.
Chemical (Corrosive)	A chemical that, when it comes into contact with skin, metal, or other materials, damages the materials. Acids and bases are examples of corrosives.
Explosion (Chemical Reaction)	Self explanatory.
Explosion (Over Pressurization)	Sudden and violent release of a large amount of gas/energy due to a significant pressure difference such as rupture in a boiler or compressed gas cylinder.
Electrical (Shock/ Short Circuit)	Contact with exposed conductors or a device that is incorrectly or inadvertently grounded, such as when a metal ladder comes into contact with power lines. 60Hz alternating current (common house current) is very dangerous because it can stop the heart.

43

Hazards	Hazard Descriptions
Electrical (Fire)	Use of electrical power that results in electrical overheating or arcing to the point of combustion or ignition of flammables, or electrical component damage.
Electrical (Static/ESD)	The moving or rubbing of wool, nylon, other synthetic fibers, and even flowing liquids can generate static electricity. This creates an excess or deficiency of electrons on the surface of material that discharges (spark) to the ground resulting in the ignition of flammables or damage to electronics or the body's nervous system.
Electrical (Loss of Power)	Safety-critical equipment failure as a result of loss of power.
Ergonomics (Strain)	Damage of tissue due to overexertion (strains and sprains) or repetitive motion.
Ergonomics (Human Error)	A system design, procedure, or equipment that is error-provocative. (A switch goes up to turn something off).
Excavation (Collapse)	Soil collapse in a trench or excavation as a result of improper or inadequate shoring. Soil type is critical in determining the hazard likelihood.
Fall (Slip, Trip)	Conditions that result in falls (impacts) from height or traditional walking surfaces (such as slippery floors, poor housekeeping, uneven walking surfaces, exposed ledges, etc.)
Fire/Heat	Temperatures that can cause burns to the skin or damage to other organs. Fires require a heat source, fuel, and oxygen.
Mechanical/ Vibration (Chaffing/ Fatigue)	Vibration that can cause damage to nerve endings, or material fatigue that results in a safety-critical failure. (Examples are abraded slings and ropes, weakened hoses and belts.)

44

Hazards	Hazard Descriptions
Mechanical Failure	Self explanatory; typically occurs when devices exceed designed capacity or are inadequately maintained.
Mechanical	Skin, muscle, or body part exposed to crushing, caught-between, cutting, tearing, shearing items or equipment.
Noise	Noise levels (>85 dBA 8 hr TWA) that result in hearing damage or inability to communicate safety-critical information.
Radiation (Ionizing)	Alpha, Beta, Gamma, neutral particles, and X-rays that cause injury (tissue damage) by ionization of cellular components.
Radiation (Non-Ionizing)	Ultraviolet, visible light, infrared, and microwaves that cause injury to tissue by thermal or photochemical means.
Struck By (Mass Acceleration)	Accelerated mass that strikes the body causing injury or death. (Examples are falling objects and projectiles.)
Struck Against	Injury to a body part as a result of coming into contact of a surface in which action was initiated by the person. (An example is when a screwdriver slips.)
Temperature Extreme (Heat/Cold)	Temperatures that result in heat stress, exhaustion, or metabolic slow down such as hypothermia.
Visibility	Lack of lighting or obstructed vision that results in an error or other hazard.
Weather Phenomena (Snow/Rain/Wind/Ice)	Self explanatory.

Appendix 3
Sample Job Hazard Analysis Form

Job Title:	Job Location:	Analyst	Date
Task #	Task Description:		
Hazard Type:	Hazard Description:		
Consequence:	Hazard Controls:		
Rational or Comment:			

www.ingramcontent.com/pod-product-compliance
Lightning Source LLC
Chambersburg PA
CBHW051821170526
45167CB00005B/2112